imagine that...

Susan Knoll

Charleston, SC
www.PalmettoPublishing.com

imagine that...

First Edition

Paperback ISBN: 978-1-64990-148-4

eBook ISBN: 978-1-64990-147-7

imagine that...

MISSION STATEMENT: TO ENHANCE LIVES BY ASSISTING OTHERS TO CAPTURE THE DREAMS THAT GOD HAS GIVEN THEM.

GOALS

- Brainstorm and write down BIG ideas
- Form personal goals - short term and long term
- Be grateful - develop gratefulness
- Create Vision Board with pictures and details

Table of Contents

DREAM

Mark 10:14 ..."Let the children come to me; do not hinder them, for such things belongs to the kingdom of God".

ADVENTURE 1

- Did you ever have a great idea?
- When you dream what do you dream about?
- Be creative, think outside the box.
- Are your great ideas and dreams the same thing?

LIST OR DRAW IDEAS/DREAMS:

- Big Ideas
- Fun Ideas
- Silly Ideas
- Wild Ideas
- Crazy Ideas
- Bold Ideas

Date :

Adventure 2

Every morning when my kindergarteners came into the classroom we started our day with this activity. Each day there was a different word. They were encouraged to write or draw what the topic made them feel or reminded them of. We explored:

* family, home, siblings, parents (blended families)
* outside, clouds, stars, the world, sunsets and dark skies
* playing, swinging, sports, building and creating
* colors and feelings
* some days there was only a blank and they filled it in
* limitless possibilities

At the end of the week, I stapled all the HDYFAs together from the week and sent them home in their back packs. Sometimes parents were amazed at what their child was really thinking/feeling.

HOW DO YOU FEEL ABOUT ______________________________

Date :

GOALS

Dreams are given to us by God. He wants us to dream, then He wants us to set a plan (called goals) to get these done.

ADVENTURE 3

- What do you want to do right now?
- What do you want to do when you are older?
- Who do you want to be?
- What do you want to have?
- Who do you want to help?

DO	BE
HAVE	HELP

Think big. List every idea/dream that you can come up with.

Date :

Adventure 4

What can you do? Imagine yourself already doing whatever you are dreaming about. Everyone is cheering you on as they see what you are accomplishing! You are making God really happy! Share these dreams with us so we can cheer for you too.

Make a list of 7 of your greatest ideas that you can see yourself doing.
Start each statement with I am....

You may use words from the boxes to help if you would like

ADJECTIVES	VERBS
amazing interesting funny quick great loved brave curly beautiful	loving helping serving munching wishing climbing sprinkling whispering building

NOUNS
brother/sister son/daughter basketball player pianist helper

1. I am
2. I am
3. I am
4. I am
5. I am
6. I am
7. I am

Date :

GRATEFUL

AN ATTITUDE OF GRATITUDE

Think of the different ways that we can pray to God about the things that we have and want to have and do. Here are some examples, what do you think?

- A prayer that says Thank You to God.
- A prayer asking God to help someone else.
- A prayer asking God for His blessings or protection.
- A prayer that praises God and says "I love you" to Him.
- A prayer that says I wish I hadn't chosen to do that.

ADVENTURE 5

1. Postcard Gratitude

Kids say thank you routinely but do not show appreciation for someone's character. Try sending 3 thank-you postcards per week to family and friends. Thank a sick friend for their bravery. Thank a relative for the service they do for others thru their job. Thank a teacher for helping them. The recipient will be thrilled to get it in the mail.

ADVENTURE 6

2. Whiteboard Thanks

Give every child a space for a mounted whiteboard. (Bedroom door or locker front) Anyone can write on it as long as the message is positive, such as a note of thanks or a Bible verse. For example: You helped me...You smiled at me...You made me feel special...

Show appreciation and encouragement.

Date :

GRATEFUL (cont.)

ADVENTURE 7

3. Thanksgiving Tree

Set up small tree. Make tags out of cardstock, punch hole in the top and tie a loop with yarn through the hole. Each day (week, month) everyone comes up with what he or she is grateful for that day. Only rule...you cannot use something someone else has already used. At the end read each tag and observe how God has truly blessed you.

ADVENTURE 8

4. Appreciation Balloons

Write an appreciation note for everyone in the family or class. Roll up the notes and squeeze them into separate balloons. Inflate and write each person's name on their balloon. Give each person the balloons with their name on it and let them pop the balloon and read their notes. Example..I had a mess and you asked if you could help me clean it up. Way to serve.

Date :

GOALS in PICTURES

let's create a vision board!

ADVENTURE 9

Materials you will need:

- Poster board or white board or maybe an old mirror
- Pencil, pens, markers or crayons
- Magazines or pictures that interest you
- Scissors
- Glue or tape
- Paper

Make a list of 5 of your ideas that you would like to do now or sometime in the future. Your desires/your dreams.

For each idea find and cut out a picture that reminds you of this. Post this on your board.

For each picture write down several details that you will need to follow to accomplish this. Example, a picture of a place you have always wanted to visit...when will you go there, how will you afford this, will you take anyone with you, what else will you see along the way?

You may want to look up and write down encouraging bible verses to use on your board. Check out some of these **or** use your own favorites.

Psalm 145:9	Numbers 6:24	Colossians 3:2	Hebrews 13:8
Psalm 150:6	Proverbs 3:5	1 John 4:19	Philippians 4:13

Date :

APPENDIX

Worksheets

BIG IDEAS

FUN IDEAS

SILLY IDEAS

WILD IDEAS

CRAZY IDEAS

BOLD IDEAS

How do you feel about ______________________________

DO	BE
HAVE	HELP

1. I am
2. I am
3. I am
4. I am
5. I am
6. I am
7. I am

Write them again and believe what you write!

1.
2.
3.
4.
5.
6.
7.

Psalm 145:9 -The LORD is good to all.

Numbers 6:24 - The Lord bless you and keep you

Colossians 3:2 - Set your minds on things above, not on earthly things

Hebrews 13:8 - Jesus Christ is the same yesterday, today and forever.

Psalm 150:6 - Let everything that has breath praise the Lord.

Proverbs 3:5 - Trust in the Lord with all your heart.

1 John 4:19 - We love because he first loved us.

Philippians 4:13 - I can do everything through Him who gives me strength.

NOTES

1. *My Idea*, written by Kobi Yamada, illustrated by Mae Besom.

2. *Dream It, Pin It, Live It*, Terri Savelle Foy, The Fedd Agency, Inc. Copyright 2015.

3. Scripture quotations taken from ESV, You Version Bible App.

4. *Peter's Perfect Prayer Place* by Stephen Kendrick and Alex Kendrick, illustrated by Daniel Fernandez, Kendrick Brothers, LLC, Copyright 2015.

5. *Focus on the Family, Helping Families Thrive*, OCT /NOV 2018 page 8, Corrine DelGallo

6. *Focus on the Family, Helping Families Thrive*, OCT /NOV 2018 page 8, Tammie Haveman

7. *Focus on the Family, Helping Families Thrive*, OCT /NOV 2018 page 8, Barbara Douma

8. *Focus on the Family, Helping Families Thrive*, OCT /NOV 2018 page 9,Linsey Driskill

9. Illustrations by Amy Knoll Fraser.

Who Am I ?

I love mountains, especially the mountain tops. I was born in WV, lived in PA until I was 10 years old, then moved to Kentucky. I always lived at the foot of a mountain. Now I am living in Johnson City, TN. I am married to my exciting husband Alex and we have 3 children and 6 grandchildren.

I am finding natural ways to cook for us and keep us healthy. My dear friend, Judie Camak, introduced me to Jamie Hyatt and Young Living Essential Oils. Yea! One of the ongoing educational adventures that has been part of my local Young Living experiences was a class that Jamie facilitated about Vision Boards, "Dream It, Live It, Pin It" by Teri Savelle Foy, creating our own Vision Board from our passions and deep desires. This was such an inspiring goal setting time!

Since, in one of my former careers, I had been an Elementary School Teacher, this took me immediately to how could we teach kids this at an age where it could shape, form, and change their lives. This caused me to put together "...imagine that". I believe you can adapt it to ages from preschool to preteens. It can be used by teachers or Sunday School teachers as a curriculum or as supplemental material. Don't forget Home Schooling. Use a few or use them all. It can be used by all parents to help them guide their child's development. For me, it is exciting to see children plan their own goals and actually see their ideas in a form that will take them through their growing years with a sense of self motivation and value. Just imagine what fun it would be growing up following your dreams.

This experience has been orchestrated by God. Without Him, this work would not exist. I thank Him for using me and the glory is His. I pray that everyone that uses this resource will be blessed immeasurably as they live, thrive and bless others!

Susan Knoll

www.ingramcontent.com/pod-product-compliance
Ingram Content Group UK Ltd.
Pitfield, Milton Keynes, MK11 3LW, UK
UKHW051206260726
13967UKWH00011B/3139

9 781649 901484